The Worship Tithe

by

Brenda Engram Salter, Ph.D.

Resolve that with reckless abandon –
"I will worship the LORD and fall in love with Him."

Atlanta, Georgia

ISBN: 0970545835

The Worship Tithe
Copyright © 2008 Brenda Engram Salter, Ph.D.

All rights reserved. No part of this publication may be reproduced or transmitted in any form or by any means, electronic or mechanical, including photocopy, recording or any information storage or retrieval system, without permission in writing from the publisher

All scripture references are from the King James Version of the Holy Bible

Library of Congress Cataloging in Publication Data

Printed in the United States of America

www.theworshiptithe.com
www.royaltybooksintl.com

This book was written under the inspiration of the Holy Spirit and is solely intended to minister to and give information to the reader to make informed decisions that will affect their purpose and destiny. Names, characters, places, and incidents are used fictitiously, and any resemblance to actual persons, living or dead, business establishments, events or locales is entirely coincidental.

Foreword

This book has redefined what we know today as worship. Rather than following others in a "worship" service, Dr. Salter has been given inspiration from God on how He wants to receive worship. Being God-breathed, this book is one of the instruments the Lord will use to bring His people closer to Himself in these last days. Dr. Salter is alongside other great people who have had experiences with God such as Spurgeon, Henry, and Chambers. She takes her experience one step further and provides the Body of Christ explicit instructions on how to enter worship to God in a 24-hour day. Once you read this book, your life truly will never be the same. Once you have read this book, your life truly will never be the same.

Blessings,

Dr. Karen L. Hypolite
Author and Educator

Prologue

9 Months until the Birthing

From August of one year to May of the next year, I continued with consistently giving God His tithe, the *worship tithe*. It was after these nine months that I was able to deliver the baby- this book was conceived! I knew when God gave me this concept that a book would come, but this is not the kind of book that can just be manufactured, it must be borne out of experience. So, after 9 months of carrying this baby, I gave birth.

A Note from the Author

"I Love to Worship"

All of the expressions of prayer are vital, but I would contend that worship is the most precious. After worshipping God on this new level — almost exclusively during the 9 months, I almost had to re-teach myself in the other expressions of prayer: supplication, intercession, etc., because I had given myself over almost completely to worship. I was not asking God for things during these 9 months. It was simply a time of just blessing God for who He is — not for what He has done.

Contents

Foreword — *iii*
Prologue — *v*
A Note from the Author — *vii*
Introduction — *xi*

Chapter One
　The Worship Tithe: What is It? — 1

Chapter Two
　The Difference in Praise and Worship — 5

Chapter Three
　Getting to Know God Through Worship — 9

Chapter Four
　Worship and God's Grace — 13

Chapter Five
　Prescriptive Worship — 19

Chapter Six
　Worship Made Simple — 23

Chapter Seven
　Lord, Teach Me How to Worship You — 29

Chapter Eight
　Waiting Worship — 33

Chapter Nine
　Give God His Word in Worship — 37

Chapter Ten
　Have <u>Thine</u> Own Way, Lord — 41

Chapter Eleven
　The Benefits of Worship — 45

Chapter Twelve
Results of Worship   49

Chapter Thirteen
The God of Reciprocity   53

Chapter Fourteen
Worship… A Lifestyle   57

Chapter Fifteen
Worshipping With/Without Music   61

Chapter Sixteen
Positions of Worship   65

Chapter Seventeen
Worshipping with a Bowed Heart   69

Chapter Eighteen
Say Words to Him   73

Chapter Nineteen
Association Brings on Assimilation   77

Chapter Twenty
Fall in Love with Jesus   81

Chapter Twenty-One
The Void in You   85

Chapter Twenty-Two
Walking in Authority   89

Chapter Twenty-Three
Counterattack with Worship   95

Chapter Twenty-Four
Reckless Abandon   99

Epilogue
"God Speaks" A Revelation During Worship   103

Acknowledgments   105
Dedication   109
About the Author   111

Introduction

The Worship Tithe
Malachi 3:10

"Bring ye all the tithes into the storehouse that there may be meat in mine house, and prove me now herewith, saith the LORD of hosts, if I will not open you the windows of heaven, and pour you out a blessing, that there shall not be room enough to receive it."

Bring the *worship tithe* into God's storehouse that there may be meat in His house – worship is the Lord's food and when you feed Him – He feeds you back – the God of reciprocity.

I know that today we typically use this scripture in reference to money, but in Bible days, it also referred to animals, grain, and land. When the Lord spoke to me regarding the worship tithe, the reference was to worship – giving God just twenty-four (24) minutes out of a 24 hour day – everyday! I spoke back to the Lord regarding this. My thoughts were that 2 hours & 40 minutes would equate to the tithe, but the Lord told me that a minimum of 24 minutes worshipping Him would promote relationship – time in His presence that would bless Him. I argued that this was such a brief amount of time for daily worship. His response to me was that I would be surprised at how many would not – even at 24 minutes –consistently give Him this kind of daily, sustained worship.

Although I have been given to prayer as far back as I can remember (three years old), this was new for me. As a child, my grandmother would carry me to prayer meetings. I have fond memories of playing with my doll underneath my Grandma Carrie's quilting frame while she and Mother Braswell quilted and prayed – quilted and prayed. I was literally "covered" in prayer. My grandmother also recognized that as she and my mother (her daughter) had a prayer anointing, I too had been anointed for prayer. So she would carry me around to visit the sick and shut-in and direct me to pray for them. At an early age, I experienced laying hands on the sick and they recovered.

Praying has been a life-long joy and lifestyle for me. Conducting monthly all-night prayer shut-ins is also something that my pastor and Bishop had put me in charge of along with one of the brethren. Being one of the intercessors for my local church was another of my assignments.

The prayer ministry is one that I have been involved in for most of my life, but this worship tithe that God spoke to me about was something I had never heard of before. Thus began my rendering to God the worship tithe, the tenth, <u>24 minutes a day- at the beginning of each day.</u>

For nine months, I consistently worshipped God for at least 24 minutes – often longer- and got to experience Him in an extraordinarily new way. How could I share this new-found joy with others unless I had experienced it consistently myself? Throughout this time-frame, I knew that I would share this experience in a book, but it was only after the nine months in consistent, one-on-one worship (private worship – only God and me) that I began to actually write the book. The birthing of what I had been carrying for 9 months was released!

My question to you is this – Is 24 minutes too much to give God? Are you willing to give God just 24 minutes out of your 24 hour day for worship? And isn't that just like the generous God He is. He always allows us to have the larger percentage for ourselves. When we give God 10% of our increase, we get to keep the 90%. But, if you're like me, you'll exceed the 10%. Because of your love for Him, it will be difficult to leave His presence. There are times that I will not want to do anything else – go to work, exercise, eat, etc., because of enjoying the fellowship, the relationship, loving on Him and Him loving on me. And because God is love, spending time with Him like this will cause you to become more loving. People can go to church week after week, year after year, and still be mean and unloving. One of the reasons is simply because of not spending time with the God of love.

Psalms 92:1-2

"It is a good thing…. to show forth thy lovingkindness in the morning; tell of His lovingkindness and thy faithfulness every night" Worship God in the morning. Praise Him before you retire for the night.

The scripture – Psalms 92:2 is in alignment with the way Jesus taught the disciples to pray in Matthew 6. In verse 9, the opening verse of this prayer, Jesus teaches them to worship- Our Father Who art in Heaven – (Abba Father is addressed.) Hallowed be Thy Name (His name is Holy, righteous,…). I believe that this prayer is in priority order. Before anything else, the first thing in this prayer is to worship. Then at the end of the prayer in verse 13, Jesus taught the disciples to praise God - For thine is the kingdom, the power, and the glory – God's greatness and glory alone are worthy of praise and thankfulness. Praise and thanksgiving recognize that everything belongs to God. The earth is the Lord's and everything therein- Psalms 24:1. For thine is the kingdom (it's Yours and we praise You), the power is yours, and the glory belongs to you – forever. Amen. And so it is! Hallelujah!

Chapter One

The Worship Tithe: What is It?

Proverbs 3:7

Proverbs 3:9 *"Honor the LORD with thy substance, and with the firstfruits of thine increase."*

The worship tithe is a firstfruit offering. Before starting your day, begin with giving the Lord the first of your day… and the tithe is holy (Leviticus 27:30). Know this, however, that worship by no means exempts other forms of prayer (supplication, intercession, confession, praise) that may follow the worship tithe or that may be rendered at other times during the day, and I did say time<u>s</u> because you may pray in the morning, at noonday, and/or at night. Or, you may designate an hour in the afternoon when you set aside that time that is devoted to prayer. Surely, as Christians, we have a praying spirit, so our spirit man prays without ceasing- prays throughout the day and prompts us to pray intermittently-throughout the course of the day.

I Thessalonians 5: 17

"Pray without ceasing."

However, the scripture Psalms 63:1 "…early will I seek thee" bears attention. God never wastes words, so there is something to be gained and said about rising early and seeking God, spending time in His presence, giving Him the tithe (off the top of the day) first! Selah.

We cannot spend time in the Lord's presence and not be changed! As we continue giving Him our firstfruit prayer – the worship tithe, we get better, stronger, wiser.

Give God His tenth – the *worship tithe*!

My Worship Scriptures

Reflections and Affirmations

Chapter Two

The Difference in Praise and Worship

There is a difference in praise and worship. Many think of these as the same, but they are uniquely different. Vine's Expository Dictionary of Old and New Testament Words renders praise as AINOS (noun) and AINEÓ (verb), while worship is SEBASMA and ETHELOTHRESK (noun) and PROSKUNEÓ (verb). When we praise, essentially we are thanking God for what He has done – and if we are honest, we are thanking Him for what He has done for us.

Now, take the following scenario into consideration: The wife comes into the room where the husband is and without her doing anything, he just begins to speak accolades about her to her: "Honey, you are so beautiful, loving, and kind. I love the way you smile – the dimple in your cheek. Not only are you beautiful on the outside but inside as well. I have it all in you, my darling – beauty, intelligence, and spirituality. If I searched all over the world, I'd find none other like you!"

Scenario #2: The husband comes in from work and before he can change clothes and prepare to cut the grass, the wife greets him and says, "Honey, you are the man of my dreams.

I love everything about you – your strength, your character, personality, good looks- you handsome hunk! You have it all – brains, brawn, love for your family and for God!"

These examples are quite different from praise- quite different from saying thanks for chores done or even for gifts given; you are the beneficiary of those. Not that we are to worship our mates, but I trust that you get the parallel. When you affectionately tell each other about the other, each becomes the sole object of the affection. So it is with God. Praise is definitely in order- thanking God for all that He has done for you, but to worship Him for who He is is uniquely different.

> Give God His tenth – the *worship tithe*!

My Worship Scriptures

Reflections and Affirmations

Chapter Three

Getting to Know God Through Worship

Getting to know Jehovah God through worship is key to understanding who you are. When you know who "I AM" is, you'll know who you are. Get to know God, and you'll know you.

If true identity of who God is is to be found, it is through worship. God is complex and so are you. I believe that when the angels bow before Him crying "Holy, Holy, Holy," it is partly because every time they rise from bowing, they view another aspect of Him – world without end. Since we are made in His image and likeness, it serves to reason that we too are multifaceted, multiplicitous.

Some of the frustrations of man are borne out of the fact that he truly is not a flat, static being. Being multidimensional like God means that we are not the same all the time. Accept the richness of which we are made.

Through worship, we get to know more and more about God and Who He really is. He reveals Himself – the very mystery and majesty of Himself – through worship. When you know who "I AM" is, you'll know who you are.

In Creation Therapy, a christian counseling clinical approach, man is studied through five different temperaments: Melancholy, Sanguine, Choleric, Phlegmatic, and Supine. I believe that each of these is a reflection of a piece of God in each of us. The clinician studies and discusses the dynamics of each of these temperaments and aspects of God. When learning about them, we can declare as David did that we are fearfully and wonderfully made. Come on and let's worship God.

Give God His tenth – the *worship tithe*!

My Worship Scriptures

Reflections and Affirmations

Chapter Four

Worship and God's Grace

Our firstfruit prayer – the worship tithe - does not negate the need for God's Grace. We must ask for grace to run this race. If we are not careful, we will think (subconsciously) that because we are worshippers, we are automatically infused with **all** that is needed to run this race, but there will be storms, tests, and trials that can only be overcome by asking God for His grace – the kind of gracing that allows man to say "no" to the enemy and "yes" to the Lord.

I Corinthians 10:12

"Wherefore let him that thinketh he standeth take heed lest he fall."

Only God's grace is sufficient for some storms, some battles, some trials, some tests, and tribulations. You cannot tunnel through in your own strength, your own righteousness, the wisdom and strength of another (mentor, leader, parent, friend, boss, sibling), but simply the Grace that God gives to those who ask for it will receive His strength, His wisdom, His Grace.

There is the kind of Grace that works with mercy in a time of need, but then there is the kind of Grace that enables us to do what needs to be done at a given time – Grace to love the unlovely, grace to tell the truth when a lie seems appropriate, grace to do the right thing when the wrong thing beckons you. So remember that although Worship is the first thing that Jesus taught his disciples to do in Matthew 6:9 – "Our Father which are in heaven, hallowed be thy name," we must never forget that it does not preclude our need for Grace – so ask for it in your time of struggle, your time of need, and you'll be amazed at how liberal God is with dispatching it. Worship will not render you a Superman or Wonderwoman, but it will strengthen your relationship with the Lord and enable you to accept His Grace undoubtedly. If you are not a worshipper, receiving His Grace may be a struggle for you. *I have known people who were Christians but were not empowered because without worship, you don't build the kind of spiritual muscle that is needed to cast out doubt and fear. The more you worship, spend time with Him, the more it is that doubt and fear are cast out.

I know of a man who was shot multiple times. Some of the bullets grazed him, but three entered him on the right side while two entered him on the left. Additionally, one of the three gunmen pointed a gun at his head apparently with the intent of finishing him off, but when this man said, "In the name of Jesus…" the gunman's hand began to shake and they all left the scene. The amazing thing that followed was that because this man was a worshipper, fear was replaced with WORSHIP.

This man, lying in a pool of blood, understanding that he would surely die (and that he surely did) began to worship. His testimony is that he began to worship as he lay there dying. The story continues: a lady with a white dress on came from out of nowhere, lifted his head and placed it on her lap and said to him, "You're going to be all right." He states that he journeyed toward heaven and experienced an unspeakable kind of love, joy, and glory. He tells how he heard the playful, joyous voices of little children and how he was at peace, but he heard what had to be the voice of the Lord tell him that he had to go back- that it was not his time. Though he dreaded returning to this world – even the thought of it was more painful than the pain he had experienced in his physical body – return he must. As he opened his eyes while lying in the hospital with tubes attached and with a doctor about to cover his face with a sheet, the doctor dropped the sheet and ran out of the room. This man further recounts that he was told he had been dead for thirty minutes – but God! Now, there are many things that can be extracted from this miracle, but the one that I presently want to focus on is the miracle of worship. In the midst of his suffering, in the midst of his pain, lying in the pool of blood, he worshipped. Fear was dispelled because when you have a relationship with Him – not an acquaintance but a relationship, you can't help but to worship. That's the kind of love that casts out all doubt and all fear.

Give God His tenth – the *worship tithe*!

My Worship Scriptures

Reflections and Affirmations

Chapter Five

Prescriptive Worship

The tithe is holy! The worship tithe is holy! Give God the fruit of your lips before you do anything for anyone else. This time must be prescriptive. If it is not prescriptive, you may worship haphazardly, sporadically, or just occasionally. But if it is prescriptive, like your prescription medicine that is taken daily, then you will have the full and proper dosage, and you're not likely to miss.

Purpose to meet with the Lord on a daily basis and at a prescribed time – preferably upon rising. You won't see all of the results after the first dose, but as you take a daily prescription of worship, you become more and more transformed into His image. You know how it is when you hang around with someone a lot – perhaps your best friend, you tend to talk similarly, laugh alike, and even sometimes dress alike. So it is with the Lord. When you spend time with Him in worship, you become healthier, more exuberant – more like Him! This is the kind of prescription that you cannot overdose on; it can be addictive, however.

Give God His tenth – the *worship tithe*!

My Worship Scriptures

Reflections and Affirmations

Chapter Six

Worship Made Simple

David was after God's heart. He sought to please the heart of God, so He sang to Him, played to Him, spoke words to Him, and danced before Him. It's no wonder that God said that David was a man after God's heart. As the dear panteth after the water brooks (David said that), so panteth my soul after thee, O God (Psalms 42:1). He was very passionate about his pursuit of God. He pursued God with <u>everything</u> that was in him.

Psalms 100:1-2

"Make a joyful noise unto the LORD, all ye lands. Serve the LORD with gladness: come before his presence with singing."

Like loving your mate, the dream of your life, love your God. He is so much more than any mate, and He deserves so much more.

Some young girls give their bodies to men who will give them money, or clothes, or jewels, or cars. They give themselves in exchange for light bill money, rent money, gas money. How much more then should we not give ourselves to the One who <u>really</u> loves us, the One who died for us, gave His life for us, the One who loves us with an everlasting love – a genuine, unconditional love. For God so loved the world, that He gave His only begotten Son, that whosoever would believe on Him should not perish, but have (inherit) everlasting life (John 3:16) – life eternal – a life of peace and joy – with no sorrow, no pain. Who wouldn't worship, serve, love, honour a God like that.

Psalms 100:4b

"…Be thankful unto Him, and bless His name."

So, how do we worship? We simply come before His presence with singing, with a thankful, grateful heart, and with praise. Be careful not to utilize the time in worship solely for praise. Praise is a part of what we do, but it is not all that we do. <u>When we worship, we must and want to tell God about Himself.</u> There are no fancy words needed. It's simple – just give Him you. He already gave you the very best He had – Jesus!

For "Worship Made Simple", follow these simple steps:

1. Tell God about Himself
2. Tell him who He is to you
3. Tell Him how you give yourself to Him
4. Speak about His
    a. Nature
    b. Majesty
    c. Deity
    d. Royalty
    e. Being Creator
5. Tell Him how much you love Him
6. Tell Him what you will do for Him
7. Tell Him about His Faithfulness
    (See Psalms 136)

Give God His tenth – the *worship tithe*!

My Worship Scriptures

Reflections and Affirmations

Chapter Seven

Lord, Teach Me How to Worship You

In the midst of your worship, when you seem to have run out of words, say, "Lord, teach me how to worship you." He will begin to lead and guide you into the kind of worship that is not contrived, that's not mundane, that's not the "same-o, same-o," but it's fresh, it's vibrant, it's spontaneous. In one setting you may just begin to sway before Him while in another you may dance. You may sing or you may just speak words to Him. Whatever the expression, you are sure to be giving God what He wants – because you asked him to teach you. It may also just be a time for "waiting worship."

Give God His tenth – the *worship tithe*!

My Worship Scriptures

Reflections and Affirmations

Chapter Eight

Waiting Worship

Psalms 27:14

"...wait, I say, on the LORD."

"Waiting Worship" is the kind of worship that invokes the Holy Spirit in your "Wait." You're not speaking, singing, or dancing; you're just "Waiting" in His presence. As the Father wraps you in His loving arms, there's a hush, a stillness, and you just enjoy the silent communion with Him and He with you. In your wait, not only is He blessed, but you are blessed. Strength comes in the wait; power comes in the wait; joy comes in the wait, patience comes in the wait; deliverance comes in the wait; your health springs forth speedily in the wait. There is such a sweet serenity found in the wait. Wait, I say, on the Lord.

Has there ever been a time when you were with the man or woman of your dreams and you didn't talk to each other audibly, you didn't do anything with each other, but just silently enjoyed each other's presence – it was intentional silence – the kind of silence that was nonetheless exhilarating. That's what is borne out of "the wait." And, when "the wait" is over, you leave feeling refreshed, revived, renewed. Wait again, I say, on the Lord. Know that during the twenty-four minutes of "waiting" in His presence, this worship tithe is holy!

    Give God His tenth – the *worship tithe*!

My Worship Scriptures

Reflections and Affirmations

Chapter Nine

Give God His Word in Worship

Psalm 66 is a good place to begin. This Psalm of David is a worship song that speaks about the awesomeness of God. The Word of the Lord says, "How terrible art thou in thy works! Through the greatness of thy power shall thine enemies submit themselves unto thee. All the earth shall worship thee, and shall sing unto thee; they shall sing to thy name. Selah. …See the works of God! You are terrible in [Your] doing toward the children of men. [You] turned the sea into dry land: they went through the flood on foot: there did we rejoice in [You]. [You] ruleth by [your] power forever; Your eyes behold the nations: let not the rebellious exalt themselves. Selah. O bless our God."

There are many other Psalms as well as other scriptures that can be spoken aloud to give God His Word back to Him in Worship.

Give God His tenth – the *worship tithe*!

My Worship Scriptures

Reflections and Affirmations

Chapter Ten

Have <u>Thine</u> Own Way, Lord

Your flesh will want to have its own way. Rather than worship, the flesh will want to spend an hour on the phone chatting about nothing.

I think about the time spent on the phone trying to reconcile errors in billing. You make the call to discuss the error and one representative sends you to another. That one switches you to another department. Then you are switched to a supervisor. That supervisor can't help, so she switches you to her supervisor.

When it is all said and done, you have spent two hours on the phone to only end up with a $46.11 credit. But our flesh needed to be satisfied. You wouldn't stop until you got what you called for – 2 hours later. Howbeit then that we can't allow the Lord to have His way? That company you were dealing with regarding the bill/credit had its way, and you ultimately got your way – but how costly. Nevertheless, we won't spend the same amount of time in worship, in prayer, in praise. Although, the minimal prescribed time for the worship tithe is 24 minutes, why not let God have His way. As we will say, "Lord, have your way with me," we will find that just as we often do with our monetary tithes and offering and exceed the tenth, so it will be with our worship tithe; we will want to give more!

Give God His tenth – the *worship tithe*!

My Worship Scriptures

Reflections and Affirmations

Chapter Eleven

The Benefits of Worship

There's a myriad of blessings – benefits that are borne from worship. Worship is the vehicle that transports you to a "zone" unlike any other vehicle. You enter into a realm when you worship that allows you not to leave empty or empty-handed.

<u>Because God is a God of reciprocity, you can not give to Him and He not give back to you.</u> Out of the realm of worship you extract precious promises that you could not have attained had you not gone there – worship. It's like mining for gold: it takes some time; you can't just rush into the mine and rush out. Mining for gold – how deeply into the mine must a miner go (worship mine worshipper must go)? How tedious is the process? While chipping away, a miner may get a little benefit of his <u>labor</u>, but to get the real benefits, the bounty – the GOLD, it takes some time, but the benefits are well worth it. So it is with worship. In order to get the Gold, you must go deeply into the presence of God. For many the "gold," the benefits include peace, joy, trust in God, faith, improved health, a healthy mindset, a transformed mind, better relationships, and

a satisfying lifestyle to name a few. The benefits that result from worshipping God are far too many to enumerate, but like Paul in Philippians 4:8 says, "…whatsoever things are true, lovely, and of good report" – those are the ones to think on as benefits that come to those who will worship God!

Give God His tenth – the *worship tithe*!

My Worship Scriptures

Reflections and Affirmations

Chapter Twelve

Results of Worship

Out of worship comes a greater desire for things of the Kingdom. When you worship the Lord – spend alone time with Him, you become transformed more and more into His image. Things that matter to Him are things that matter to you. The most important things to Him are souls. Your desire for souls intensifies. You become so acutely aware of how important it is to go after souls. You begin to ask for strategies to win souls to Him.

There is a dying to one's self when you worship. Worship causes you more and more to shift the focus off of yourself. If you love God properly, then you do love yourself also and you are going to take care of self, so there's no need to think of others, your needs will go unmet. In fact, as the old cliché' goes, "If you take care of God's business, He will take care of yours." Do you really believe it? If so, then get to taking care of things that matter to God most: souls, feeding the hungry, clothing the naked, visiting the sick. It becomes more and more your heart when you chase after the heart of God. These are the kinds of results that come from worshipping God. You develop a kingdom- mindset, and that is one that is concerned about what God is concerned about.

Give God His tenth – the *worship tithe*!

My Worship Scriptures

Reflections and Affirmations

Chapter Thirteen

The God of Reciprocity

God desires our worship. He created us to worship Him, but I would venture to say that it is what many do least. Because God is the God of reciprocity, if we give God what He wants – worship, He'll give us what we need: joy, happiness, peace, fulfillment, love, health, wealth, relationships, decreeing power, authority, boldness – everything we need and more. "Delight thyself also in the Lord; and He shall give thee the desire of thine heart" (Psalms 37:4). Needs will be met when you worship, but you can also get your heart's desires when you worship. You can not worship this reciprocating God and not receive from Him when you give to Him.

Give God His tenth – the *worship tithe*!

My Worship Scriptures

Reflections and Affirmations

Chapter Fourteen

Worship… A Lifestyle

When you resolve to make worship a lifestyle, know this – that you will have to fight to be consistent in this time of prayer. You will eventually strike a rhythm, but the enemy (Satan) doesn't want you to worship since he never ever will again. The enemy will try to block your worship – any way he can. Just when you begin to worship, the phone rings, the baby cries, the dog barks, the alarm rings – anything to keep you from worshipping. If you and your husband [or wife] were spending intimate time together, you wouldn't stop to answer the phone, etc. So, why should you during this time of intimacy. The (worship) tithe is holy. Then you must deal with your own schedule and your flesh. If you don't resolve to make worship a lifestyle, it will appear that you don't have time with your busy schedule. You have to leave for work too early or stay too late. Assignments and projects won't allow you to "squeeze" it in. Then you have to deal with your flesh – you're too sleepy in the morning as well as at night.

You must resolve to make worship a lifestyle. You must be convinced that your schedule, interruptions, and your flesh must not take precedent over worship. Just as everything else that you do is a part of your lifestyle, worship must be as well. Make it a priority.

Give God His tenth – the *worship tithe*!

My Worship Scriptures

Reflections and Affirmations

Chapter Fifteen

Worshipping With/Without Music

There is nothing wrong with worshiping with music. In fact scripture relates numerous instances when the worshippers called for a minstrel. There are musicians and singers who can usher you into the very presence of the Lord – and that's good. But if we are not conscious of it, we could be just swept along as when the ocean tide comes in and shifts the sand. The sand gets affected by the waves, but it isn't changed. If we're not on a conscious level aware of what happens during worship , with or without music, we will be swept along by the tide of worship, will have a an exhilarating experience – but not necessarily a life-changing experience. So, we may worship with those skilled and anointed to usher us into His presence, but we must also make it our business to go before God without the accompaniment of other voices and instruments.

Believe it or not, worshipping without music and CD's, etc, can enhance the worship experience when returning to worship with music. If you only always worship with others involved (via gospel singers, singing, and music), the level of intimacy that can be achieved without those will not be realized.

Worshipping with gospel music and songs put to music via CD can be enrapturing such that it can end up being just an enjoyable experience. It feels good at the moment, but you can leave with the greater benefits; you can often leave this kind of "corporate" experience finding yourself still the way you've always been: empty, indecisive, lonely, powerless, discontent, weak, unknowing, not knowing His voice, His will, His ways. But when you spend alone time in His presence, your life begins to change – you look different, act different, believe differently. You become powerful, empowered, content, happy, joyous, fulfilled, directed, <u>strengthened</u>, knowing his will, his ways.

We say things like "Lord, you mean more to me than life itself." But in many cases, that is just rhetoric because if it were true, could not we just commune with him alone for 24 minutes – unaccompanied by the outside trappings, the outside enhancements, the outside noises- in many cases. I'm reminded of Peter when Peter said, "Lord, I'll die with you," yet he could not pray for the 1 hour that Jesus had asked him to. Jesus said, "Could you not pray for one hour," when he returned and saw that Peter and the other disciples were asleep. Can we be alone with him in prayer for 24 minutes (the worship tithe) and not be carried by instrumentation and the assistance of what it brings to our worship experience? I encourage you to examine what your true experience really is when you worship privately and corporately – with and without music.

Give God His tenth – the *worship tithe*!

My Worship Scriptures

Reflections and Affirmations

Chapter Sixteen

Positions of Worship

Change Your Position in Private Prayer Worship

In order to avoid becoming "religious in prayer," change your position. In one setting, your position may be kneeling for that entire time of prayer. The next time, you may be lying prostrate. Then, when you worship in the next setting, you may be walking around. David even danced before the Lord. There are those who only dance before the Lord publicly, in a corporate setting, at church. But at home alone, dance before Him, twirl, rock, spin, kneel, sit, stand. Enjoy the freedom of changing your position in worship.

Change your position physically as well as attitudinally. Your attitude of worship must change. If you have been worshipping out of duty, ritualistically, or legalistically, these are all the wrong attitudes. If your position in worship has been that if you worship, you can get something from God, then that's called manipulation. Of course, you cannot give to God and not receive – simply because you can never beat God in giving; it's a part of His nature. He is a God of reciprocity – a reciprocating

God He is. So when you worship Him, great benefits you receive, but your position should not be that. Your position should be borne out of cultivating relationship – your position should be a loving one – one that has at its best the desire to bless God! Hallelujah!

Give God His tenth – the *worship tithe*!

My Worship Scriptures

Reflections and Affirmations

Chapter Seventeen

Worshipping with a Bowed Heart

Worshipping in your private time can be done with a bowed heart and your eyes open. Often when you're alone and there are no other distractions, if you close your eyes, your mind may drift off; the eyes of your soul may begin to examine things of the soul. One of the purposes of closing your eyes in church during prayer is to close out distractions – looking at other people, observing their expressions, movements, etc. This way, everybody is arrested – heads are bowed and eyes are closed. But when alone, it is a good thing to open your eyes, lift your head, and hands, and kneel in reverence before God. The position and condition of the heart are of utmost importance here, however. Worshipping God with a bowed heart signifies a reverential love, fear, and respect.

Give God His tenth – the *worship tithe*!

My Worship Scriptures

Reflections and Affirmations

Chapter Eighteen

Say Words to Him

Say words to the Lord. As my pastor says, "It is impossible to speak two languages at the same time." By the same token, if you're speaking Words to Him, you can't at the same time focus on other things even mentally. Speaking to Him audibly in worship will shut down your mental conversations. So, open your mouth and say words to Him. Saying words out loud to the Lord can bring you into an extraordinary experience with the Lord – you talk to Him and He talks back to you. This will demystify the experience; it will take the "religious mysticism" out of your worship.

There is a euphoria that many expect to be shrouded in when they worship. Without it, they don't feel that they have had a good time in worship "Oh, I had such a good time in my morning worship today. The Lord really met me," many say. But what does that really mean? It is conceivable that it means there was an emotional experience, but not a true relating to the Lord. It's ok to have an emotional time during worship, a euphoric experience during worship, but you must not confuse those experiences that may or may not render real communing with the Lord. When one has had the <u>real</u> communing with the Lord, although He is your focus, you will leave the experience different, more and more conformed to His image. You change. Your faith increases. Your attitude changes. Your belief system changes. They may be subtle changes and sometimes overt, but you cannot spend honest and true time with worshipping the Lord and leave unchanged – you cannot remain the same. The peculiar thing that happens during this "alone time" with Him is that although you are there intent with purpose to bless Him, He blesses you back. He pours into you. He makes deposits in you. Everybody's going places to have others make deposits in them – and that's not all bad, but it cannot be with the exclusion of an expectation and even longing for the great deposit that only comes from Him. So, open your mouth and say words to him and listen for Him to speak back to you.

Give God His tenth – the *worship tithe*!

My Worship Scriptures

Reflections and Affirmations

Chapter Nineteen

Association Brings on Assimilation

The adage "birds of a feather flock together" is true. Your similarities are noticeable. Have you ever noticed that after years of being together many husbands and wives look like each other? They not only begin to look like each, but often they will also take on characteristics of each other: idiosyncrasies, choices in foods and beverages, etc. I have had several very close friend girls and in most cases, people would say, "you and she talk just alike. You even laugh the same." You may adopt many other codes of life similarly. Even the way you think will be in common. That's why it is so important to choose close friends carefully.

Well, how much more do we then begin to look like the Lord, act like Him, walk and talk like Him when we spend time with Him! You say what He says and do what He does – the more quality time that is spent with Him. Your associating with Him has caused you to be more and more like Him. "Association brings on assimilation." As you will give God the worship tithe, you will become more like Him.

Give God His tenth – the *worship tithe*!

My Worship Scriptures

Reflections and Affirmations

Chapter Twenty

Fall in Love with Jesus

I recall the day and the hour that I said to the Lord: I'm in love with you. Aforetimes, I had said, "I love you, Lord." I had sung many songs that said the same. I had even sung the song that said, "Falling in Love with Jesus is the best thing I've ever done." But, I was just singing a song that someone else had written. As heartfelt as I sang it, with as much passion as I sang it, I realize now that at the same time, I was aloof. That might sound paradoxical, but nonetheless true; it was not my song. You can sing a song, but not have made it "your" song. The song is beautiful, the melody sweet, but it still had not become "my" song. Understand that during this time I was saved, sanctified, Holy Ghost filled and loved the Lord, but one Sunday morning I was worshipping and out of my spirit I said – I'm in love with you, Lord! When I heard what I had said, I began to laugh out loud. And I said it over again – and again – I'm in Love with you, Lord. I laughed again. I had an epiphany. For the first time, out of my heart of hearts, out of my spirit, the depths of my soul, I said it – I'm in love with you, Lord. This declaration just rose up out of me unaware, but it connected. I became acutely aware that this experience was one that was borne out of my having been transported from euphoria to a deeper, more meaningful relationship. I not only loved the Lord, but I was now "in love" with Him – and consciously aware of being "in love."

As I fore-stated, there are two different states. If you've ever been in love with someone, you too can attest to this difference. You can love many people; you can love your spouse; but you can be in love, and that transforms a relationship. Knowing that your mate is in love with you and not just loves you is the ideal in relationships. So, the day that I said to the Lord – I'm in love with you – transformed our relationship. He had always been passionately in love with me – He died for me – that exceeds just loving an individual. You have to be in love to lay down your life for someone – wouldn't you agree? So, He was always in love with me, but now our relationship was deepened because I was now in love with Him – consciously.

How did I come to this place? It was discovered through worship. During the worship tithe – and the tithe is holy - I came to this place. Being faithful to our relationship – spending time with Him – not defrauding Him of the "tenth," my heart strings were pulled. You can't honestly spend this kind of time adoring our Lord, saying words to Him, singing songs to Him, telling Him how absolutely wonderful He is and not fall madly in love with Him. The deep kind of intimacy that comes from daily personal worship (this bears repeating – personal worship) can only be achieved through personal worship.

Our carnal man will resist this kind of lifestyle – a lifestyle of give the Lord a daily tithe - but if you will resolve that you will, your life will change and you will be fulfilled. When you are in love with Him, you look forward to giving the Lord His tenth – the worship tithe.

Give God His tenth – the *worship tithe*!

My Worship Scriptures

Reflections and Affirmations

Chapter Twenty-One

The Void in You

Every man was created with a void in him – a cavern, a reservoir, a hole, an empty place – a place that's only reserved for the Lord. Nothing and no one else can fill that place but Him. Man becomes hungry, thirsty, lonely but can never be fully content, satisfied, fulfilled without filling the reservoir with the Lord. The interesting thing is that it can't be filled on just one occasion; there has to be a daily meeting at the watering hole.

I'm reminded of when I lived in Elizabeth, New Jersey. Near where I lived was a huge reservoir. Whenever we experienced dry spells, the reservoir would dry up and become empty. I would go for walks alongside the reservoir, pushing my daughter Erika in her stroller. I would notice how barren and cavernous the reservoir was without water. I also understood the ramifications of that. Without water in the reservoir, the potential for suffering increased. That reservoir was purposeful in supplying our community life. The fuller it was, the greater potential for life; the drier it became, the less potential for life. I was so thrilled when on my strolls, I saw the reservoir full, flowing, full of life-giving water. We too can flow and be full of life when we have the life-giving water flowing in us. How do we get full? How do we fill the reservoir of our souls? How do we quench this thirsting, satisfy this hunger? WORSHIP. Sex, drugs, family, friends, jobs, food, alcohol, money, sleep, entertainment, cars, houses, education, mate, husband, wife, girlfriend, boyfriend: none of these – no one and no thing - can fill the void that was on purpose created in us by the Creator but Him. This place was created by Him to only be filled by Him.

So, if you aren't worshipping the Lord – giving Him what He deserves – what He wants – you will not reap the true benefits that can only come through <u>Worship</u>. You will remain empty and craving things that will not satisfy. The void, however, can be filled through daily worship. Now come on and worship Him.

♪ Fill my cup, Lord. I lift it up Lord. Come and fill this thirsting in my soul. Bread of Heaven, feed me, till I want no more – Fill it up and make me whole.

Give God His tenth – the *worship tithe*!

My Worship Scriptures

Reflections and Affirmations

Chapter Twenty-Two

Walking in Authority

God honors a worshipper in innumerable ways. One of the greatest ways, I would say, is that of walking in authority. Walking in authority metaphorically is the overarching umbrella, and under it are all the "goodies" that come from walking in authority: fearlessness, boldness, to name a few.

As a result of developing a relationship with the Lord through worship, one of the great rewards is becoming so insulated in His presence that you develop a fearless nature. You begin knowing without a shadow of a doubt that – no weapon formed against you can prosper. Without being steeped in that knowledge that comes only through worship, that scripture doesn't fully come alive in you. You will have a "head" knowledge of that scripture, but chances are you will not have the reality of that word operating in your life.

After the fall of man with Adam and Eve, sin came into the world and separated us from God. After receiving salvation, what a travesty to still be separated because of a lack of communion that only comes through worship. We cannot operate in our

God-given authority if we don't know who we are in Him. Psalms 8:5 indicates that we are just a little lower than God Himself. The true revelation of that is revealed in worship. We know that the scripture says this, but we walk around with a poor self-image and low self-esteem, underestimating who we are and that we are <u>more</u> than conquerors! As we spend time in His presence, we begin to discover more and more Who He really is which in turn helps us to discover who we really are – made in His likeness and in His image. Wow! That's powerful! And we, too, are powerful! Worshippers get to know, understand, and experience what carnal Christians don't. Adam and Eve were already as gods. Satan was successful at deceiving them by offering the idea that if they ate the fruit, they would become – who they already were. How do we rediscover who we really are? How do we take dominion and walk in authority – Worship is the vehicle that transports us there. Satan uses subtle means to cause us to buy in to the fact that we are powerless – that he is greater than we are. The more we worship, the more we are transformed into the Lord's image and walk in authority. Think on the Jehovah's of the Bible and as He is, so should we be. Jehovah Jireh – the Lord who provides; then we become like Him – providers. Jehovah Shaloam – the giver of peace; we should be walking in peace, peace givers, and peace lovers. Jehovah Rophe – the God who heals. As a worshipper walking in authority, we don't feel inferior – we speak to sickness and disease and tell it, "Mountain, be cast into the ocean."

When Adam walked and talked with God, communed with God, I dare say worshipped God, he exercised his dominion; he walked in authority. But, when He listened to the wrong voice and disobeyed God, he hid from God; he stopped talking to God such that God had to look for Adam… "Adam…Where are you?" Does God have to look for you?

Is He saying _____(put your name on the line), Where are you? because you have ceased communing with Him or because you never really became a worshipper? Just as you're not an athlete because you workout or perform a physical activity occasionally, likewise, you're not a worshipper when you occasionally worship. Makes sense? Step up in your worship; give God the tithe and you can honestly say that you are a worshipper. You can also take your rightful place and walk in authority. Begin exercising yours today if you are a worshipper. If you aren't, you can begin the adventurous journey now!

Give God His tenth – the *worship tithe*!

My Worship Scriptures

Reflections and Affirmations

Chapter Twenty-Three

Counterattack with Worship

You'd better know that when you make a decision to consistently worship [not out of duty but out of love – not for form or fashion but because God deserves it], you are going to be under attack. Satan was a worshipper before he was flung out of heaven. He can never resume his position of worship; consequently, he wants to torment those who worship the Lord. So, he will attack you in your finances, your health, your children, your relationships, your job, your belief system, your faith, your convictions. Not only does he not want you to worship the Lord, but he wants you to bow to him. If he can attack you in the areas that mean so much to you – you may 1) lose trust in God so that you won't worship and/or 2) you'll be so pre-occupied with fixing those things that you won't take the time to worship. It's happened for many in just these ways time and time again. I was speaking to a counselee about worship who was dealing with a failing marriage. My question to her was "Where is God in your life? Are you a worshipper?" She admitted that though she considered herself a worshipper, since getting married she had shifted all the attention on her husband and now on her failing marriage. She stated that she was completely oblivious that she no longer worshipped. Her days were consumed with trying to fix their marriage: praying about it, soliciting the prayers of others, going to counseling, catering to her husband in every way she could or in every way he wanted. All of her attempts were to no avail; he still wanted out of the marriage. She was feeling frustrated and unfulfilled. Heightening her awareness of what was going on or not going on in her worship life caused her to shift her focus back to its proper perspective. Her husband had become her god. The Scripture says – "Thou shalt have no other God before me. God is a jealous God." [Exodus 20:1]

Later she told me that when she began to give God a worship tithe, her life literally was changed. And though her marriage was still under attack, she now was being equipped (through worship) to handle it. At the time of this writing, her marriage was still in trouble, but she was experiencing unparalleled fulfillment that only comes through worship.

When you resolve to worship, you may experience attacks from every side, but you can worship with no money in your pocket or pocketbook. Worship will usher you right into the very presence of the Lord – where nothing else matters. Now that's a place we should all long to be, and when we reach that destination – where nothing else matters – all that previously mattered – matters to God. When you exit your time in worship, you don't exit empty-handed. You exit with solutions, power, strength, answers, supernatural ability, healing. The attacks may come and as real as they may be, your counter - attack is worship.

Give God His tenth – the *worship tithe*!

My Worship Scriptures

Reflections and Affirmations

Chapter Twenty-Four

Reckless Abandon

What is worshipping with reckless abandon? How is it achieved? It comes through destroying everything in you that is detestable to God. How can we truly worship God when there is idolatry in us, hatred, jealousy, envy, strife? In II Kings 9, God anointed Jehu through Elijah. God told King Jehu <u>to destroy</u> all of Ahab's priests and all who had allegiance to Ahab. Jehu also destroyed the temple of Baal. He was completely obedient. As a result, II Kings 10 states that the Lord promised that Jehu's descendants (to the 4th generation) would reign over Israel. As we will destroy the temple of Baal and idolatry in our lives, we will be unencumbered, free to worship God unimpeded with reckless abandon.

Resolve that with reckless abandon you will give the Lord a worship tithe – daily. Not only will you bless him, but you'll bless yourself. When you resolve that with reckless abandon you will worship the Lord, nothing else really matters – everything else pales by comparison – your worries diminish; emergencies are no longer emergencies; storms lose their effect; sickness and disease have to bow. Try it – try worshipping the Lord with reckless abandon and see what happens. The results will be unparalleled!

You'll be able to see clearer; hear (in the Spirit) more acutely; love God and man more deeply; be victorious in all areas of your life. The more consistent you are, the more the transformation happens. You'll wake one day and realize that you are not the same. The change will probably be subtle until you have been made over – afresh, anew.

When you give God the worship tithe daily, He begins to make you aware of so many things that will aid you in living the victorious, overcoming, abundant life: resources, information, knowledge, wisdom, ideas, visions, direction – all reserved for true worshippers.

Don't limit yourself and the results that come from personal worship to only that of corporate worship at the church on Sundays. Give God a worship tithe daily – reckless abandon – right in the middle of the flow of life – without striving for it, without struggling for it – just jump in – and allow the Lord to literally blow your mind! This is my experience; allow it to be yours. Those with whom I've shared this kind of experience – the daily tenth in worship (no less than 24 minutes or your 24 hour day) have testified that it has literally changed their lives. That can be your testimony as well.

God Bless!

Give God His tenth – the *worship tithe*!

My Worship Scriptures

Reflections and Affirmations

Epilogue

"God Speaks"

A Revelation During Worship

While in Worship, the Lord revealed this to me:

Look at the earth and all of its splendor — how majestic it is. Well, you are equally majestic. I, God, made the earth and all that dwell therein [Psalms 115]. You came from the earth, so you are just as majestic. Stand tall like the largest oak tree, strong with roots that run deep — you too are rooted and grounded. Run deep and wide like the great Grand Canyon — God had put depth in you — you were made from the earth. The God who created the heavens and the earth, created you.

So, reading audience if you receive this revelation for yourself, you will have no problem with self-image, self-esteem. Your Creator created you magnificently! Bless God!! Worship the Creator — Elohim — the All-Powerful Creator of the Universe!

Acknowledgments

"No man is an island, entire of itself; every man is a piece of the continent, a part of the main."

From *Meditation 17* **by John Donne**

I know far too well that I could not have accomplished the things that I have without the rich deposits that so many have made in my life. There is a song that says, "I need you, you need me, we're all a part of God's body. Stand with me, agree with me,… You are important to me, I need you to survive."

My journey began with my siblings – Cynthia, Ronald, and Alphonso. What a joy it is to have siblings that truly love. Each of them has been a source of inspiration, love, and support. When we were children and had to line up to receive punishment for some error of our ways, I would get to the end of the line and cry for each of them through their spanking. We cried together, and today we laugh together at fond and not-so-fond memories.

My extended family is a very close-knit one and one of which I am so very proud to be a part. Many of them are also in ministry and love the Lord. When attending family reunions, we always include several worship opportunities. It is great being biologically connected with worshippers.

I remember all of my pastors, their wives and families, as well as the churches I attended from childhood to adulthood. What a rich heritage to have been and continue to be among those who are sanctified. Bishop and Sister C.J. Hicks, Elder and Sister C. Demps, Elder and Sister Walton, Elder and Mother Robert L. Braggs, Elder and Sister Williams, Bishop and Mother Whitlock. Although I am pastoring now, I acknowledge my pastor Bishop Bobby R. Henderson and Lady Henderson. They were instrumental in taking me to the next level in worship. My spiritual family could never know how much they have blessed and enriched my life. It is an awesome thing being spiritually connected with worshippers.

My godson – Pastor Travis Jennings, and spiritual son – Minister Eric Martin, I love you. Thank you for your love and support.

I value and thank God for saved friends that love God and love me. Thanks Linda, Lois, Joy, Sheilda, Evelyn, Terry, Eugenia, Cynthia, Shirley, and Camilla. I believe that God ordained this sisterhood and has richly blessed us.

To my church and congregation at Restoration International Ministries (RIM), I honor God for you. You have been a tremendous blessing to me and my family. Ambassador Bernard Strozier, my first member (other than my family) as well as my long-time friend and godbrother – what would I have done without you over the years! The RIM family, you are great!

What a privilege it is to pastor you and to worship with you from week to week. God bless you and keep you, make His face to shine upon you and give you peace.

Last, but certainly not least, praise, honor, and glory to Alpha and Omega, the beginning and the end, the first and the last – my Everything! It is because of you that this book is and that I am. I love you and am madly in love with you.

Dedication

This book is dedicated to the memory of my dear grandmother, Carrie Jackson Brooks. Her example of prayer taught me at an early age what it means to be constant in prayer. She recognized God's hand upon my life, and at ages 3, 4, and 5, she took me around with her to visit the sick and released me to pray for them – and they did recover. I would also attend prayer meetings with her. Many times when my siblings were out playing, I would sit underneath my grandmother's quilting frame while she and her prayer partner, Mother Braswell, would quilt, sing, and pray; I was literally covered in prayer.

I dedicate this book to my mother, Amy Brooks Engram and to the memory of my father, James W. Engram who were parents that believed Proverbs 22:6 – "Train up a child in the way he should go, and when he is old, he will not depart from it." They were loving parents in the home and they carried us (not sent us) to church. We were in Sunday School, Sunday worship service, YPWW, and Sunday night service as well as weeknight services, Bible study, prayer service, and revivals. It was rare for me to get to watch an entire episode of my favorite television show "Mr.

Ed – The Talking Horse" on a Sunday evening because we had to return to church for YPWW before "Mr. Ed" ended.

My father was a deacon and Sunday School Superintendent. Although I loved seeing him worship the Lord, I was also embarrassed by his Holy Ghost mannerisms when he would jump and throw his leg out when dancing before the Lord. My mother was an Evangelist Missionary at that time and continues to do ministry today as Jurisdictional Supervisor in the Church of God in Christ. Who would have known that I would go on to follow in both their footsteps as a Superintendent of the Sunday School at my local church and that of an Evangelist Missionary as well. My mother has been my greatest cheerleader, role-model, and spiritual mentor. Her sterling example continues to impact my life to this day.

I dedicate this book to Ellis Salter, the father of all three of our darling children. He has been one of the best fathers a child could have. And to my children – Erika, Brooks, and Brielle – my joy! I thank god for children who love, honor, and respect God and their mother: that would be me (smile). They have added life to me through their support, encouragement, laughter, and tears. I am better because of them.

About the Author

Brenda Engram Salter, Ph.D.
Evangelism, Healing, Deliverance, Prophecy, Counseling, Preaching, Teaching Ministry

Having a legacy of prayer, with the prayer mantle passed from her grandmother and mother to her, Pastor Salter feels that consistency in prayer is essential. At a young age, she sang, played piano, ministered to the orphaned, and prayed for the elderly.

The proud mother of three, Erika, Brooks, and Brielle, Pastor Salter raised them to "get their learning and keep the burning." She has earned a Bachelor of Science in Education, a Master of Education degree, and a Ph.D. in Clinical Christian Counseling. She is a high school teacher and an adjunct college professor. She is also a licensed clinical pastoral counselor.

Pastor Salter's trial sermon was delivered in 1982 at Holy Mountain Church of God in Christ in Rahway, New Jersey under Elder Robert L. Bragg. She served as Shepherdess in the pulpit of Dr. Bobby Henderson and Anointed Word Evangelistic Tabernacle COGIC in Lithonia, Georgia and as one of Bishop Henderson's Administrative Assistants. Most recently, she founded Restoration International Ministries, Ltd, a global outreach ministry where she is the pastor. Her testimony is that she loves the Lord and the Lord's people.

Dr. Salter conducts empowerment seminars and charm and etiquette workshops. She additionally is a fashion coordinator and commentator. Dr. Salter is founder/CEO of ARCA Enterprises, Inc. She is sought after for education and women's conferences and does also conduct revivals. Her international ministry has taken her to the motherland, Lagos Nigeria, West Africa. Dr. Salter presently resides in Decatur, GA.

"Before I formed thee in the belly, I knew thee… and I ordained thee a prophet (my spokesperson) unto the world."

Jeremiah 1:5